K is for Kissing a Cool Kangaroo

For Mary – G.A.

For Pam and John Hodgson, salt of the earth – G.P-R.

ORCHARD BOOKS
Carmelite House, 50 Victoria Embankment, London EC4Y 0DZ

ISBN 978 1 40835 038 6

First published in 2002 by Orchard Books
This edition published in 2017 by the Watts Publishing Grou
Text © Purple Enterprises Ltd, a Coolabi company 2002 coolabi
Illustrations © Guy Parker-Rees 2002

A CIP catalogue record for this book is
available from the British Library.

Printed in China

Orchard Books
An imprint of Hachette Children's Group
Part of The Watts Publishing Group Limited
An Hachette UK Company
www.hachette.co.uk

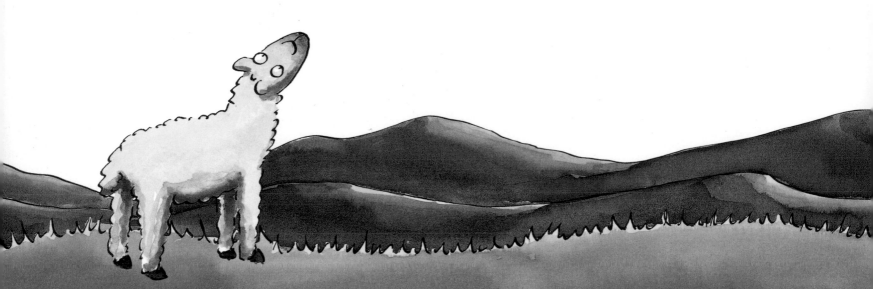

K is for Kissing a Cool Kangaroo

Giles Andreae • Guy Parker-Rees

ORCHARD

d is for **dragonfly**, **daisy** and **dream**

e is for **elephant**, mighty and strong

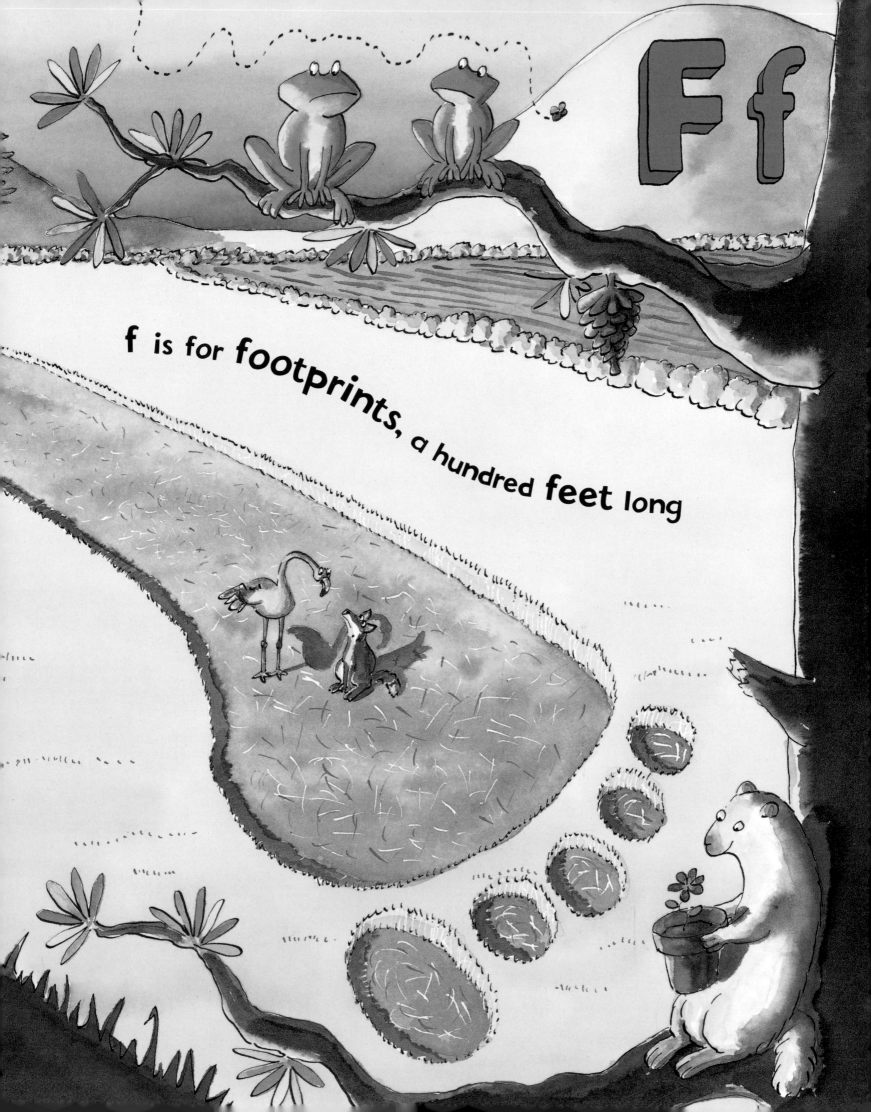

f is for **footprints**, a hundred **feet** long

Gg

g is for **giant**, whose **garden grows** wild

H h

h is for **holding** the **hand** of a child

i is for **igloo**, a house made of **ice**

J is for **jellybeans** – ooh, they're so nice!

K k

k is for **kissing** a cool **kangaroo**

l is for **loving**, like Daddy **loves** you

m is for **mischievous monkey** and **mat**

o is for **octopus**, arms everywhere

P is for **peaceful** and **piglet** and **pear**

Qq

q is for "Quickly, I've cuddled the Queen!"

r is for **robot** and **racing** machine

S s

s is for **snowman** and **sister** and **snake**

t is for **teatime,** so let's have some cake!

Uu

u is for **uncle** and **udder** and **up**

V is for **vampire** with blood in his cup

Yy

y is for **yeti** and **yoyo** and **yes**

and **Z** is for **zebra** - now how did you guess?!

There are lots of other things on every page you may have missed.

See if you can find them . . . then check them on this list!

Aa

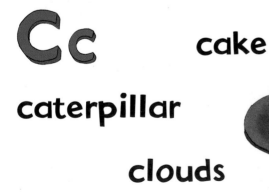

armadillo

antelope

ant

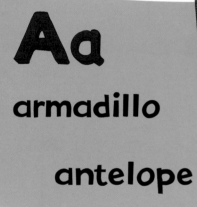

beetle

bull

balloon

Bb

Cc

cake

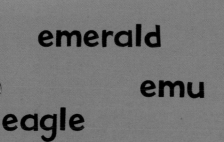

caterpillar

clouds

dalmatian

dog

duck

Dd

Ee

emerald

emu

eagle

frog

ferret

flamingo

Ff

Gg

giraffe

goat

gnu

Hh

house

hamster

hyena

Ii

icicle

iguana

ibis

Jj

jester

jaguar

jam

Kk

koala

kitten

kiwi

Ll

llama

ladybird

lynx

Mm

milk

mango

mole

Nn

nectarine

newt

nest

Oo

olives

owl

otter

Pp

pelican

porcupine

pirate ship

Qq

quiche

quail

quiver

raccoon

rose

Rr

rat

Ss

skunk

seal

salamander

toucan

Tt

teddy

turtle

Uu

unicorn

umbrella

vulture

violet

Vv

vole

Ww

weasle

woodpecker

wombat

Xx

x-ray

Yy

yak

yellowhammer

Zz

zinnia